ALMOST

OBSCENE

Almost Obscene
FIRST EDITION

Text copyright © 2022
Fondo de Cultura Económica

English translation copyright © 2022
Katherine M. Hedeen & Olivia Lott

Printed in the United States of America
ISBN 978·1·7348167·6·1

DESIGN ≈ SEVY PEREZ
COVER PHOTOGRAPH ≈ MILCÍADES ARÉVALO
Brandon Grotesque & Adobe Caslon Pro

This book is published by the

Cleveland State University Poetry Center
csupoetrycenter.com
2121 Euclid Avenue, Cleveland, Ohio 44115-2214

and is distributed by

SPD / Small Press Distribution, Inc.
spdbooks.org
1341 Seventh Street Berkeley, California 94710-1409

A CATALOG RECORD FOR THIS TITLE IS
AVAILABLE FROM THE LIBRARY OF CONGRESS

ALMOST

OBSCENE

RAÚL GÓMEZ

JATTIN

translated by Katherine M. Hedeen
& Olivia Lott

CONTENTS

[He looks out the door of his house and sees the police lieutenant]

86

[The devil is a bat that stows away]

87

[The dark wizards got into his brain]

88

["I am your mother listen to me in your mind]

89

["I am your big brother" he says deep down "I am eternal]

90

[In his skull the dead father's voice thinking]

91

["I am your sister the witch   I am a witch]

92

[Lying on the sidewalk watching the stars]

93

[A bunch of kids all around him]

94

[The threat has been carried out:]

95

["I am Satan   You are my legitimate son]

96

["Listen to Levián the painter of angels]

97

I WAS LIKE WEED but they didn't smoke me

I HAVE FOR YOU my good friend
a Sinú River mango heart
fragrant
true
kind and tender
(What's left of me is a wound
a no man's land
a stone's blow
a blink of an eye
in a faraway night
hands slaying ghosts)
A word of advice
don't come across me

YOU TRY TO SMILE

and a bitter sigh brews
you mean to say love but say far-off
tenderness but teeth turn up
exhaustion but tendons tear
Someone raises solitudes in your chest
nails
tricks
ditches
Someone
your brother in death
captivates you   catches hold of you   drives you mad
and you   defenseless
write him these letters

WHAT COULD YOU POSSIBLY remember Isabel
of the hopscotch beneath your patio's mamoncillo tree
the ragdolls that were our children
the railing where all the boats from Havana would dock filled with…
When you had golden eyes
like peacock feathers
and skirts stained with mango
Forget it
you don't remember
I on the other hand   you couldn't tell today
No one's said anything
I keep throwing pebbles into the sky
looking for a place to rest my feet before I get too tired
Tracing and erasing shapes in the skin of the earth
and my children are rags and my dreams are rags
and I keep playing dolls in the spotlight on the stage
Isabel peacock eyes
now that you've got five children with the mayor
and a fancy chauffeur to take you around town
now that you wear glasses
when we see each other you shoot me a quick "how's life"
cold and impersonal
As if I still had one
As if I still had use for one

I LOVE YOU LITTLE DONKEY
because you don't talk
or gripe
or ask for money
or cry
or make me slide over in the hammock
or get all emotional
or sigh when I come
or frown
or grab me
I love you
all lonesome
like me
No expecting to be with me
sharing your pussy
with my friends
No making me look bad in front of them
and no asking me for one single kiss

BEAUTY TOOK ME OVER
just like you'd take a boat
or a city
From its captive pleasure
my ordinary life
trembling These poems sobbing

DEATH WALKS IN YOUR BONES
and blossoms from your skin
so you offer me
a rose
whose petals
fall
Infinity rain

THE WORSHIPPING GOD

I'm a god in my town and my valley
It's not because they worship me   But because I do
Because I bow down before anyone who offers up
some passion fruits or a smile from their own garden
Or because I head down to the bad side of town
to beg for money or a shirt and I get it
Because I keep a close watch on the sky with my sparrowhawk eyes
and then talk about it in my poems   Because I'm lonesome
Because I slept for seven months in a rocking chair
and another five on some city sidewalk
Because I give wealth the side eye
but I'm not mean about it   Because I love anybody who loves
Because I know how to grow orange trees and vegetables
even in the dog days of summer   Because I have a compadre
whose children I baptized and whose marriage I blessed
Because I'm not good in a way people get
Because when I was a lawyer I didn't defend capital
Because I love birds and rain and its wide-open
washing my soul   Because I was born in May
Because I know how to sucker punch my sticky-fingered friend
Because my mother left me right when
I needed her most   Because if I'm sick
I go to the free clinic   Because basically
I only respect those who respect me   The ones who work
every day for their bread bitter and lonely and wrangled
like these poems of mine I've stolen from death

MEMORY

Beyond death and its devastations
keeping on like life unscathed
there's a sun home to doves and trees
It watches over your future halfway through my childhood

Joaquín Pablo   my old man   old friendly kid
Age mixed us up and tore us painfully apart
On May mornings waiting for rain
and in hours of sun and rooster
scuffle squabbling in the brush

There's a grave silence like oblivion
It clouds my eyes and crushes my throat
in your voices that I hold onto like a warm blanket
for the yearlong cold and worn loneliness

You were the last honest man to survive happily
You were that sensitive sower of loving passions
Halfway through life your body got away from me
Sunny cautious like a tree laden with mangos
handed down to me in the sickest part of my soul

SMOKE ABOVE THE AIR

I've never met my brother Miguel
He's here to put me to sleep in my hammock
Clear honey eyes and meat-eating smile
Broad body just right for neglect
Like all of us he smokes to keep his hands busy
and above the air smoke traces
some sort of bad luck sign
My mother didn't cry the night he died
Before he vanishes with the smoke I think
maybe I would've loved him

HUSTLER LOOKING IN THE MIRROR

He knew how to get by on his beauty and smile
His sensual youth a female in bloom
Lazy
Didn't like thinking or working
He lived off men

And men came and went
like a train over a soft animal
leaving only a scrawny old cat
A pathetic broken-down shadow

Now feeble with spotted skin and sad eyes
how it must hurt to look in the mirror
long for what's lost
Cheap glory eaten away by life
returning each night in dreams
begging for you to remember

THE DEALER IN WORDS

You lived off her
Didn't pay her what you owed her
Life led you to other things

Distracted you forgot your Muse
and she wandered
Never put her worth on any altar
Terrible enemies:
Her sullen face makes for dry mouth
Feeling strangles
Her lonesome movements clouding your soul

Now you wish   Dear one
you hadn't hurt her so bad

THE MAN WHO NEVER UNDERSTOOD

An indifferent witness
You didn't get it
Didn't help the victim

An accomplice to betrayal and ignorance
You deliberately accepted
the man wasn't worth it

When they took him to slaughter
you were close by
but just squandered hostile glances

When they asked you
if that friend in his poems was you
you fiercely denied it

Now that you live among ordinary things
do you forget that glorious time
when poetry was at your feet?

THE ONE WHO WON'T LOVE

Snow from years on end
dropped down from your hair to your pupils
You were left blind
and then almost voiceless

Punishment of life
for who thought it could be fooled
by luck

Punishment of love
for who used lies
and slander
as weapons

Punishment of death
she'll be on your bed
but you won't see her coming

TANIA MENDOZA ROBLEDO

Woman with an elsewhere kind of beauty
You had to cross the sea
to find love

You left us Petulia almost forever
and almost none of us realized
how caught up we were
in our own pathetic lives
to understand your love affair

Woman with hushed dark flesh
Companion
None of us knew how to hold onto you
You were never really there
From then on you went your own way

A tragedy waxing on stage
like a moon
like a love potion for our eyes
seeing her and never sated by her beauty
burning away over some lousy
rotten oak planks
Tania Mendoza Robledo
Brilliant tragedy of the Colombian stage
That bitch
died each night like a coraguala flower

and gave off a scent of sadness
to anyone with the terrible luck
of gazing upon her

Wherever she is I picture her performing
something supposedly modest
something that scarcely matters to anyone

MISUNDERSTANDINGS

Oh unlucky parents
Such a disappointment in your distinguished old age
your youngest son
the smartest
Instead of a respectable lawyer
a renowned pothead
Instead of a loving husband
a guarded bachelor
Instead of children
some poems in need

What horrible sin did this respectable old couple
commit? Was it beyond words?

The truth is as a child his father told him about freedom
How Honoré de Balzac was an extraordinary man
Recited Canción de la vida profunda
Not knowing the mistake he was making

URBAN POET

That poet from Bogotá
As a boy he never knew
the scent of wet earth
or the revealing touch of animals
or saw the river wash life away...

To make up for so many losses
he sets a bird free in every poem
Clouds come and clouds go
At each sunrise the sea
swells tides toward his forgetfulness

That poet
grows quiet when I write to him
about how man's most pressing tragedy
is his war against nature
He writes long poems
to a papier-mâché lover

You're no match for the flowers
Yours are tinplate stars
Your scenographic sea
doesn't reveal or give rise to memories

Poet
You must go to nature
To gaze upon it
To defend it

EASTERN ABUELA

Abuela dreamy
fresh from Constantinople
Evil woman
who'd swipe my last piece of bread
Mythical monster
her womb swollen
like a giant pumpkin
I hated her as a kid

And still she's come back
this tragic night
with a kind of beauty
There's a reason people say
with time you can forgive almost anything

She's come back with her soul scarred
harem fugitive
sounding "shit" in Arabic and Spanish
With her lonesomeness in those two languages
And the vague glimmer on her back
of a tall Syrian sprig

THEM AND MY ANONYMOUS BEING

It's Raúl Gómez Jattin to all his friends
and it's Raúl Gómez nobody when he walks by
When he walks by everybody is everybody
Nobody's me   Nobody's me

How can those people love me
if Raúl is nobody   That's what I think
If my life is a gathering of them
as they go through its middle and make off with my sorrow

It must be because I love them
Because my heart's divided up among them

So Raúl Gómez lives in them
Crying laughing and occasionally smiling
Being them and sometimes being me too

CERETÉ, CÓRDOBA   *for Zuni Roca*

Maze of farewell witnesses to tears   Sun
So much sun sometimes I've forgotten its nights
Sun on rooftops and pedestrians rushed
But also shade below the sky sombrero
Shade in the park's fig trees   And sometimes
sweet shade in what a friend says

Maze chased by my same old childhood
With purple doves in the bell tower
and in the hands of children when the virgin Fátima
showed off her incredible pureness in a cotton dove
the size of a house   It seemed to smile
And the thoughtful miracle of doves set free
from our hands   Do you remember Zuni Sara Thelba
Rosalba Manuela María Auxiliadora Narcisa Daniel Joaquín
      Susa Martha?
Remember?   You all flew toward her   And cooed to her

Alba do you remember when you dressed up like an angel
and your wings fell off?

A river that cools the sun's glare and memory
splits the town in two   And it's meek like the good Ceretanos
Since there's another kind too

34

I loved Love twice there
And one time Love said yes
And another time it said no
No fucking way
I had a house there with a straw roof
And holes on top
where wind would slip in to bring me
news of the Universe

I had a family there who loved art and nature
Now with my folks gone we're running loose in the world

I dreamt of writing and singing there   I dreamt of taking Cereté
Córdoba with me to other places   Spelling it all out on a blank page
so people from somewhere else could discover the nights starry
with fandango sperm in the Candelaria
And your kind-hearted souls my friends
you know how to promise the moon
with a bottle of downed white rum
I love you all even more in exile
I remember you with a sob soon to burst
from my moonstruck throat   Here's the proof

ANSWER TO A LETTER

When your letter got here babbling like the wind
I'd already thrown all the books out on the street
and since mine wasn't there I threw myself out too

I'd wandered around the sad bitter blushes
of those poor men who'd watched me grow up
like a tender beast writing and dreaming
Those people from a place I love
upset and uneasy with me turning out a poet

I begged for spare change for my poems
and I offered them my life spiked with sorrows

I sang on the sidewalks and fell for a lover who was cruel
but beautiful like an evening star in the death night

In my heart you're the poet who taught me
with your wisdom and calmness to read poetry

Admired and distant   Jaime Jaramillo Escobar
Still friend and brother to my loneliness like my own poems

INESCAPABLE NEED

Álvaro   I put up with a river of sickness and death too
in my geography and loneliness   Álvaro Mutis
Isn't it true we have to let these rotting waters
flow so life and poetry come up for air?
That we must look death in the eye
to learn to die alone?

You've taken root in my same old feelings
I would have loved you even if I didn't admire you
I would have let you get close
if I'd seen you on the street one day

You in the "blinded well" of exile know
a man doesn't hand over his friendship but
for an inescapable need   Here's all of it
Hold onto it like a handkerchief
that's just soothed some tears

I BEG A DEITY

I caught misfortune making off with my doves
so I scared her away with a thrashing
She came back teeth trembling with rage
and stole my passion with a slap to the face

Forgive me lady dark and venerable
for my bastard son boldness
I can't go on anymore with an empty heart

METAPHYSICS OF POETRY AND DEATH

Get up
like you hadn't died
Get up and look
like you'd never died
at who's writing these poems

Blue right?
Blue and white
Split by a violet ray
Two hands   One mouth
And almost all the rest

I am
one more dreamer
my love

FACE TO FACE WITH A DARK MIRROR

Like a still current stained with oil
it shimmers and darkens an image I can't make out
Face to face with a dark mirror I'm still a young man

Those can't be my eyes   Much too beautiful
to be mine   I don't have that kind of glow
don't have those eyelashes lit up by youth

My early baldness is gone   Same with
all the swelling from forty years lived
in solitude and madness   My mouth
busted in its sweet intimacy won't admit the pain

My nose and chin show off a balance
they've never been able to keep   with a kind of Apollonian shadow

This mirror is something like life's pimp
Like a kindhearted hustler giving me a wicked thing

HIDDEN ASSAILANT

Life poisoned me
Took away my natural movements
and handed me over to the shadows
of unreciprocated loves
Toyed with my dreams
wedged itself like a conniver between its cracks
Dusted off memories
that dealt with goings and goodbyes
In the meantime my soul
already used to bad luck
saw it all happen
like a prisoner witness to
the gallows raising

I DEFEND MYSELF

Before devouring his thoughtful innards
Before insulting him with words and gestures
Before knocking him down
Credit the madman
His clear talent for poetry
His tree branching out of his mouth
roots tangled in the sky

In his sensitivity painful like birth
we are laid bare to the world

SPELL

The folks from my village
say I'm a dangerous
wretched man
And they've got a point

Dangerous Wretched
Poetry and love did this to me

Ladies and gentlemen
Stay calm
I usually just
do damage to myself

PRAISE FOR HALLUCINOGENS

From the *stropharia* mushroom and its deadly wound
my soul gleaned a hallucinated madness
to give my same old words
all the decisive sense of life

To sweetly vouch for my loneliness and its causes
Get up close to the mule of my old anguish
and pull from her mouth all the zeal possible
all the slime and gently strangle her
with poems knotty from grief

A different praise
for those endless teenage years
granted by cannabis   Its evil isn't as beautiful
But thanks to its sickly spell
visions came back to my writing once more
Certain lovers returned vested in eternal
glow   Some childhood passages spilled
their lightness unbroken onto the page   Same old
deceptions showed me their guts

Some folks will have faith in art for a lifetime
the intelligent cold of its reasonings
I go kowtowing from tear to tear
Gather tender syllables laughter undenied
But to revive it in the sure chance of a soul resting
Not its idleness

I go from hospitals to jails to familiar places hostile
like them   Souls with hypodermic faces
and charity beds   Giving up my company
in exchange for an awful bone of food

I owe my whole wonderful life to hallucinogens
Soul fragility isn't about taking
something on for its own sake   It's about the contempt for the sore
bloody like the banquet of Thyestes
Lopsided excess offers it up futile and for nothing

MAY THE GIRLS FORGIVE RAFAEL SALCEDO

I'm about a woman and a man   Broken
by a tender virility   My soul overpowered
by a feminality hardened on art
And still I've always loved a friend more

I've had women I love at my side
I offered Tania my heart on the stage
And we spoke
on the Bogotá streets and beneath the Cali night
My bones rattled before the clearness
in Margarita Bermúdez's honey-colored grape eyes
My poems in Beatriz Castaño's voice and music
are the feelings of a heart like mine

But a friend is a friend and I hope the girls can forgive him
They don't put up with all my boozing like Rafael Salcedo
Like my sweetheart Rafa Salcedo Castañeda
Harmony in a soul maleness
like the vast cool breeze of the Universe
They don't put up with so much mooching like
good old Rafa friend for life
Ciénaga's celebrated   Beautiful tragic
like a bird caught in the storm

SHE FEELS SORRY FOR HERSELF

I would have liked to be a man
to own you
Knock each other around as a sign of love
and loyalty
Slip on my cowboy boots
and ride you naked
Threaten you at gunpoint

But me
A woman
Just a woman
How can she make her mark
when she goes after love?

OUR HAMMOCK

Come out to the hammock where I wrote
the book devoted to your sacred presence
It reminds me of all that loneliness
I put to sleep in it   All my soul motions
tracking flight to words
recording the rain of your tears
in a less fragile time   The dreamed serenity
in your chest   The morning I'll always remember
when we held hands through all the chaos

In that hammock womb I laid down
my exhaustion with life   Rocked the pains
Defended myself from the dog days of summer   And dreamed:
You'd come to soothe me in the middle of the night
and I said that   I'd write a poem to keep
your memory safe and I did   Untie my sad wings and I cried

Lie down and let me rock you so you cool off
Try to sleep   I'll watch over you

FOR STENDHAL

Love has crystallized three times
HENRI BEYLE STENDHAL

He came contraband   Crawled through the windows
of my soul like the new year sun
And caught me so young   So devoted to him
and so free at once   He came and said his name
Laid hold of me with the wings of his voice and I was his bird
Pushed me gently toward the shore
Heard me speak of small things told in trust
We kept each other warm like orphans all alone

Another time he showed up with the voice and accordion
of the Zuleta brothers   We got drunk
just off looking at each other   Just off our sneaking around
I feel so loved when I'm next to this man
He feels nostalgia and sorrow   He loves happiness

Saying goodbye he blew me a kiss
with the palm of his hand   And I returned it   And now
I'm as much his as I am mine

THE LAST SHOT IN THE MILKY WAY

In my deep masturbation sky
you're the space of unbreakable insatiable desire
Devoured tender tireless by your sex
even if you have no idea   Your body lives in mine
It's as much mine as it could never be out there
in the real world   It's mine when I want you
In the same endless unreachable way
this book is yours   The way I am yours

We live in the eight   Dual infinity
of two universes   Circle 8
Like two twin stars
Two eyes   Two asses close
Two testicles kissing

When you get to my sky I'm naked
and you like to rest on
the pillars of my legs
My middle dazes with its force its erect flower
and my cave carnal gnostic like Plato's
Here you slip away toward the other life

In this sky you give into what you really
are   Kiss aggression   Sword clashing
Gasp smashing like the sea against my chest
Madness in your Eastern eyes brightens

the orgasm daybreak while your hands
keep hold of me   And you tell me
what I want and breathe deep
like you were being born or dying
While semen rivers swell
and flesh shakes and triggers its pleasure
toward the last shot in the Milky Way

On our sky sheets there are clouds
scent of underarm and soft residues
of love   On the pillow your head's left
a hollow that smells like jasmine
And in my body and soul the deep sorrow
of knowing you despise my love

Only for you was my life reborn
in death's glow

"EL AMOR BRUJO"

I stole some of your body and soul
Laid a trap for the memories
I'm retelling you here   Do you remember my love?

The nearly blue night sky glimpses out
from behind your eyelashes   Night trembling

Once I went up to your part of the forest
sick off mushrooms and sorrowful sorrows
And I hallucinated your tall supple figure
galloping on a cloud horse   Later
in the evening you came from Retiro de los Indios
in your white carriage and I went along
the highway on foot   Like a sleepwalker

You smile from far off like you're chewing
my heart with your fangs

My words strip away your dead life
You go on living in this book even though I'm scared of you
Even though we've barely spoken   I still love you
as much as always   As much as you can imagine

And we're so distant   Like sun from sea

THE SAILBOAT IN DREAMS
DRIFTING PAST A CASTAWAY

Steadied in your genital voice   In the carriage spinning
at full speed pearl and rosy that takes me to where you are
with cottonfields and birds and sacred zebus   There goes
my illusion of a shared future body to body
the fatal facts of our story and the time we won't get back
flow over me like a glass of sexual poison

What more could you—blood brother—even want if now
you're inside me and what I write   As if you were
my last breath   The sailboat in dreams drifting
past a castaway

I'm not yours but I'm not mine either   I belong to the
moments where you sometimes take up space   Still
the wound is all yours   So is the sorrow that assumes you'll forget me

NAVEL MOON

I sketch your outline from the lighthouse down to the city walls
Your iron eyes are glow hallucinated
Sea skips over stones and my soul's got it wrong
Sun sinks into water and water is pure fire
You're almost like a dream   Almost a stone in time's swaying

A tender archetype solid in these dim days
your way of soothing my tears
Letting loose your body against mine   Mad
like a foal in prairie fire
Spilling your words on my knowledge
like a poison to heal absence
Recalling things used and forgotten
with a bright wondrous flight

It's getting late my love   Sea brings storms
A pale moon recalls your navel
And a few clouds light and slow like your hands
drink thirstily   Like when I die up against your mouth

ALMOST OBSCENE

If you'd like to hear what I say to my pillow
your face blushing would be enough
They are words close like my own flesh
It feels the ache of your cruel memory

Do you want me to tell you?   You won't use it against me
        some day?   I say:
I'd kiss that mouth slowly until it turned red
And then to your sex the miracle of a hand going down
at the most unexpected moment to brush against it
as if by chance the same intensity swaying the sacred

I'm not wicked   I just want to make you fall in love with me
I'm trying to be honest sick as I am
to fall under the curse of your body
like a river fearing the sea but always dying in it

SERENADE

Come to the window love
the sky's sparked a fandango
in its distant bend   And it's not so cold

In the trees wind sets a moan to music
It sounds like you tuned in to my pleasure
looks like you leaning over my face
whispers signs to me along the way
"Not yet" or "Hurry up I can't wait"

Come to the window and stop being scared of your father's Colt 45
I've brought my own

Can't you hear me?   Don't you want our love
to last one more day beneath the stars?   Like gods
Didn't you slip your old man some Valerian in his coffee
so he'd fall asleep and leave us to what's ours?

I begged you like that and you had nothing to say   Later on
I found out they'd sent you off on vacation to Paris
days before   So you'd forget about me   The town
poet   The one who'd earned a sad
reputation as a fag from your beloved body
Don't forget none of that matters to me
It's just jealousy   Just nonsense from your old man

and his boring friends pussy tormentors
and from those fake friends of yours who like my dick

Don't forget that love's worth more
than all of them put together   We've even fought
against ourselves   Our pleasure
has all the masculine beauty they've never known

THE SOLITUDE OF GÓMEZ JATTIN

My love I don't know where you're burning now
I need to surrender you as always like a slave   Poor you
You've got to fall ill again and again .

What to do with you there all empty
like foolish biology   Come on get rid
of your grief and take flight

What does this moment tell you? Do you like that aged
attentive way your beautiful niece looks at you?
Go and bring her back to when she cried for no reason
Or when she wet her pants from laughing so hard

Or better yet go roam an open field and plant a grand tree
Or get yourself a rope and a pocketknife
make a kite and use it to raise your loneliness
to the clouds

No   My friend we really don't want to do any of that
We want to lie down again over her belly
But those times have passed   Her body and desire
wander between movie theaters and city bars
feverish after other bodies and other desires
And that's okay   It's her life without us
She too has the right to open pleasure

There's the moon abandoned and it's not dying   The wind is lonely
You've got me
And Our Lady   The Solitude of Gómez Jattin

THE PRINCE OF THE SINÚ VALLEY

His feelings more airy than heron wings
and still as solid as their flight   His virility
a proud masculine prince arrogant dreamer   Carries
himself like he can't help but love   His land
the earth   Mythical zebus white and reddish
A carriage of wood and dark violet metal
Like his eyes   Where he holds the Damascus night
His voice thunder watered down by the whisper of a breeze
Elegant like a desert horse   His ways
vestiges of Eastern ancestors smoking
hashish   The blackest eyelashes flicker the air
purple deep under ancestral addict eyes
He lies down on a pistachio-green silk cushion
Feeds on almonds   Olives   Rice
Raw meat with onion and wheat   Unleavened bread
Raisins   Sesame   Coconut   Tart yogurt
His colors black   Blue and magenta
His elements air and land   His spirit
like a young peasant god pushing away the harsh winter
To grant his strength to the countryside's weak   His intimate
essence the eternal boy within
the poet's illusion and his mad wanting to reach him
in his full short-lived journey toward manhood
Well-known to unhappy habits

His sense uncontested an arrow a heart pounding
from the sorrow of erotic bliss   His pleasure a full spilling
of the self over my dreams forsaken in his hands
His forever in me like a long-desired love
at the heart of every moment   Of every poem

ON WHAT I AM

In this body
where life grows dark
I live
Soft belly and balding
A few teeth
And me inside
like a convict
Inside and in love
and old
I decrypt my hurt with poetry
and the outcome is mostly painful
Voices announce: here come your sorrows
Voices crack: now your days are gone

Poetry is our one companion
Get used to her sharp edges
She's all you've got

A PROBABLE CONSTANTINE CAVAFY AT AGE 19

Tonight he'll go to three dangerous ceremonies
Love between men
Smoke marijuana
And write poems

Tomorrow he'll get up past noon
With a busted lip
Red eyes
and another enemy paper

His lips will hurt from having kissed so much
His eyes will burn like glowing cigarette ends
The poem won't reveal his tears

NOT ONE SWEET NIGHT

This fevered love tortuous   This waiting
for the moon amid coconut palms   Just in case she'd
bring me signs of your body   But nothing
But I was too sick to stand
the closeness of your touch   You would've known
nothing in me but the poet tremble and his death

This fear of eye contact it wasn't in vain
You were covered in another world   Far off
Mostly when I loved you   When I was
yours like a cloud mirrored in water
Inside but distant   Within the womb
of a made-up reality gone just like that

Wholly beautiful because I left your body
untouched though we didn't want it that way
But before my desire came my future
You before my desire for you
before desire came love
Before love came life and its wickedness

This love never had a single night
Not one sweet night my love

PRIAPUS IN THE HAMMOCK

When I met you I was coming back from the dead
Dead and veiled in my own memories
Back from hiding in a heavy madness
that grabbed hold of my life and offered it to the wind
to be taken to some sightless place   far off
free of things that look like life
to lock it away at the cost of our spirit
Free of the bad luck of bitter and alone

When I met you even the sun was my enemy

Words ran away from my voice

I'd gone so many nights hands untouched
mine ached frozen to the bone

Now you're right here in the closeness of my hammock
stretched out like a sleepy priapic faun
the body of your masculinity surrendered

I don't love you so much but I need you more than this poem

from *On Love* (1988)

MENKAURE

The golden rowboat slowly navigates among water lilies
as Nubian dancers try to cheer him up
but the Pharaoh's thoughts are absorbed
in dark omens and he pays them no mind
His soul screens almost everything around him
and he only hears the paddling of the oars
and only sees the ibis birds fly over the river
The pyramid's almost done
and its truncated top can be made out in the distance
There Menkaure's embalmed mummy will be buried
For now he's smiling distracted
at his sister and wife the Queen of the Three Egypts
He's read The Book of the Dead
He's consulted the priests of Osiris
Isis and Thoth for oracles and premonitions
and they've assured him he'll live many more years
But the building is stone by stone
and it seems the tomb never progresses
Will I—Menkaure wonders—manage to die at the right time?

THESEUS

Mary Renault—the night in the labyrinth
with muddy floors reeks of blood
from the victims the monster killed
throughout his years of infamy
The passages open onto doors
open onto other doors and onto other doors
They all end at the tip of the horns
of the one who owns this death kingdom
Day—if it even arrives—shines over
the blood flowing from the latest boy
who lies stretched out and dies slowly
The palace is a perfect snare for crime
—Jorge Luis Borges—the entrance is also the exit
Stairs always lead to nowhere
Spaces look the same and constantly
threaten with a fake way out
But the beast is witless—my Friend
and with the help of the woman and poetry I've figured out
the mystery of the path and I've killed it
I've killed it—I've killed you my friend
when I understood the labyrinth your body has
kept like a snare for my desire
I've told your muscle it makes no sense
I've built a house from your body
where death lives inside

MEDEA

Medea sharpens her knives in the palace kitchen
with a fierce wildly twisted smile
with a ruthless murderous intent already put
to the test when she quartered and boiled her father
the king of her own native barbaric land in a pot
It's been three days since she poisoned the gifts sent
to her rival the doomed princess promised to Jason
They're burning poisons meant to destroy flesh
Sly Medea brought them over from Colchis
Now Medea—Euripides' Medea   Medea the murderer
      good old Medea—
the job done she goes from kitchen to bedroom
filled with see-through tulle and a bed lofted like an altar
and hides her knives under white sheets
made of virgin wool brought from Micenas and Rodas
She's reflected before a tall silver mirror
fixing her headdress of pearls and dark amethysts
arranging her bangs on her forehead
admiring herself all calm
and carefree despite her terrible plot
She smooths out the creases in her heavy robe
sewn with radiant Assyrian gold thread
She from beyond Hellespont has no fear
When she surprised her sleeping father
everything was ready and went according to plan

Now with her children as her sweet victims
their defenselessness and love for her makes it even easier
for Medea's plots to turn out like she thinks they will
On the balcony her flying carriage waits for her
led by fire-breathing dragons
Suddenly her bright panther-like eyes ignite:
she's heard her children's familiar voices
Moving carefully she goes to gather the knives
Grabs them with a practiced quickness   Hides them behind her back
      and waits

ROXANA

She'd never before seen a man more beautiful than him
with his golden skin and night-like eyes
with his perfect godly body
She'd never met someone so cultured
He tells her wise things she otherwise
never would have imagined or known
and treats her so honorably that Darius
—her father—looks out of place and uncouth at her side
Still in spite of it all she longs to return
to the Persepolis gardens or to the beach
at Ormuz or to her desert palace
for at times in the middle of the night she'll catch
the man she loves—Alexander King of Macedonia
and now Persia too—leaving
the bed where he's loved her
for the bedroom of his friend Epaphroditos
who waits for him naked and drunk off wine

ANTINOUS

Small soul
Fickle heart
Magnanimous
HADRIAN

My master the Spanish Emperor is a man held dear
Yet he's just as terrible as he is loving and good
since power bestows an almost unbearable charm
Though I really ought not to complain even one bit
about Hadrian who's wiser than wise men
knows my land even better than I do
the Greek gods like a Greek man
understands all cultures like
no one else   And loves me madly
He's founded a city in my honor
I bring lotus lilies for our garden
and I trapped a Nile bird myself
They are gifts I entrust to him with my whole soul
With any luck his lovestruck memory will hold onto them
Still after giving them to him I am saddened
since he receives so many a day
Sometimes I fear losing his love
I'd rather drown myself in the river
May the gods take pity on my seventeen years
I so ignorant fragile small
have a lover who owns the world

SCHEHERAZADE

She's in love with the killer who forces her
night after night to wring out her memory
for the next twist in her long ancient tale
to save her defenseless life just for a moment
And while Scheherazade tells tale after tale
the Caliph kisses and holds her lustfully
and she's to keep entertaining him with her storytelling
since the executioner awaits each dawn
She's at the mercy of the one who listens spellbound
but won't lift her death sentence
Artists always have a mortal enemy
to weaken them in their endless work
to forgive them and love them each night: themselves

MOCTEZUMA

The Quetzal birds fly around their golden cages
The jaguar a gift given to him by a Toltec Prince
roars in the well made of jade stones
La Malinche combs the straight hair
of the King of the Mexican nations and the ones beyond
their borders with other names
The face of Quetzalcóatl in polished silver
is friendly though he seems to forewarn
something dark ahead for all Aztecs
Both know they only have twelve moons left
before the prophecy is mercilessly carried out
and the Feathered Serpent appears
after five hundred years of absence
with his myth incarnated in a white man
to whom Moctezuma will surrender his rule
If the lovers only knew that in the distance
crossing the Sargasso Sea
Hernán Cortés and his soldiers were on their way
planning to raid and murder
they would take up arms to defend and save themselves
or they would plan a wise escape
But no—Myth is the undisputed heart
of History and lucky Hernán Cortés
will be received as if he were Quetzalcóatl
to shamefully kill Moctezuma

LOLA JATTIN

for Alejandro Obregón

Beyond the night twinkling in my childhood
Beyond even my first memory
is Lola—my mother—facing a wardrobe
powdering her face and fixing her hair
She's already made it thirty years beautiful and strong
and she's in love with Joaquín Pablo—my old man—
She doesn't know I'm hiding in her womb for whenever
the strength of her own life needs mine
Beyond these tears running down my face
her immense sorrow like a stab wound
is Lola—dead—still vibrant and living
sitting on a balcony to watch the stars
when the swamp breeze messes up
her hair and she combs it once again
with some sort of concerted laziness and pleasure
Beyond this instant gone and it won't be back
I'm hidden in the flow of a time
that takes me far away and now I can sense it
Beyond this verse that's killing me in secret
is old age—death—everlasting time
when both memories: my mother's and mine
are just a lonesome memory: this verse

from *Children of Time* (1989)

BUTTERFLY

I am a convict
in a prison of health
and I find myself unfaded
Find myself happy
like a butterfly
just born
"¡Oh quién fuera hipsipila
que dejó la crisálida!"

I fly towards death

PORTRAIT

If you want to know about the Raúl
who lives in these prison cells
read these painful poems
born out of grief
Bitter poems
Poems simple and dreamt-of
grown like grass grows
between the cracks in the pavement

BIRD 2

In the mental health clinic
I live a piece of my life
I get up with the sun there
and in the meantime I write
my pain and sorrow
without sorrows or pains
In my ataraxic spirit
my heart flashes
like a butterfly
in the light and then darkens
like a bird when it gets
that there are iron bars
locking him up

POETS MY LOVE

Poets my love are
a bunch of horrible men a bunch of
lonely monsters   Stay away from them
at all costs   Starting with me
Poets my love are
just to be read   So don't pay attention
to what they do in real life

from *Butterfly Splendor* (1993)

HE IS LYING ON THE SIDEWALK

His soul gone
His sensitivity here
Can't get to sleep
His face on the back of his hand
Hopes for even the tiniest bit of rest
People speed by in their cars
Stars shine for the wretched one

What to do this fatal night?
Try to sleep
Forget about being out in the open

His feet brush against pebbles
in his awkward open-air bed

Will the devil come tonight
with his enchanting conversation?
Or will it be Jesus back to tell him off
to say he's the worst man in the universe?

WHY SO CRUEL TO THE POOR MOTHER?
Not a word to her for six years
If he wasn't convinced that she'd
betrayed him
—casting spells to make him go mad—
why stop saying hello?
His canine pounds from unrelenting remorse
soul suffers
Oh! He grumbles in the dead of night
Such is my misfortune! Woe is me!
He knows he's under a spell and cast out of paradise

TO WAKE UP SUDDENLY AT THE BRINK OF DAWN

sense the devil in the corner of the room
Arm and leg hair stand on end
in true terror
Hear deep in your brain:
"We are the black wizards" "You are under our spell"
Hear the white wizards: "Go shave off
your eyebrows mustache and hair
Hurry up There's no time Just
a few minutes to do it"

He flips on the light and grabs a razor
quickly gets rid of the hair on his face
before sunrise
Finished he hears the mother's voice trilling:
"Hijo How'd you sleep?"
The white wizards speak in the brain silence
"Don't answer: it's all her fault"
Silence

GOING INTO THE BATHROOM BETWEEN
HIS ROOM AND THE MOTHER'S

he yells out love songs
He sings to kill the mother
by giving her a heart attack
The white wizards put him up to it
He sings for almost half an hour and the mother doesn't die

Water floods the bathroom and seeps into nearby places
Silence
"Hijo stop singing already   Shut off the water"
says the mother from the living room
No answer
He goes out to the living room and sees the mother leave
Naked he goes to the door
and watches the mother go into the house across the street
He can't kill her with love songs!

THE SCENT RISES FROM HIS BODY   Smells like hell
In his brain the white wizard voices:
"You smell like a rattlesnake   They've slipped
the poison into your coffee"
It is a death scent   Smells like the devil
"Go put some cologne on your bald head"
says the voice   he does
For a moment the rotten stink fades
"Let's get ready to die bravely"
he thinks   but death doesn't show up

"YOU WON'T DIE" THE DARK WIZARDS WHISPER

"You'll bum around sidewalks   beg for food"
He's seen lying on the sidewalk
Covered in flies his head muddy
chewing on a few bitter roots
"God" he pleads "Tell me, what did I do?"
Waits for an answer
But God must be busy
"God" he presses on "it's me the wretched artist"
"What did I do to deserve such suffering?"
Silence

THE DARK WIZARD VOICES SOUND LIKE A SHRIEK
feminoid and caustic
Say in the deepness of his thoughts
still with diabolic beauty
Say in rhythm and short bursts
Force him to listen
Amid the voices the devil's:
"You are my daughter artist" It sneers
"If you can't defend yourself
that's because you're a sissy"
His feelings are hurt but there's nothing he can do

HE LOOKS OUT THE DOOR OF HIS HOUSE
AND SEES THE POLICE LIEUTENANT

speed by:
Looks like a black dog with eyes on fire
Thinks he smells like burnt semen
The lieutenant yells at him: "I'm the devil"
He slams the door in pure panic:
What if the devil comes back? What then?

The maid shows up she's smiling
She has a tail tipped with a poison dart
"Sir" she flirts with him "Don't you want some breakfast?"
The white wizards whisper:
"Don't eat anything   It's all been poisoned
Don't lie down don't doze off
If you lie down your spine will be crushed to pieces
If you fall asleep the devil will take you away"

THE DEVIL IS A BAT THAT STOWS AWAY
the stars   Flies over him and laughs at him
with enormous blood-stained jaws
"I killed God"   He shouts
"I keep him in hell nailed
to a fire cross   Thousands of fire crosses
I'll show you"
He's in the park and from there
he can see the hell womb
Thousands of Jesuses crucified blazing
in flaming iron cells
"Oh daughter of mine! You'll be there someday"
Insult again helplessness again

THE DARK WIZARDS GOT INTO HIS BRAIN
They carved up his insides with the sharpest scalpels
"You are a woman" They yelled and laughed
He felt a sharp pain in his head
He begged all night but nobody heard him
"We're doing surgery
When we're done you'll be a different person"
The pain hurt him infinitely
But the dark wizards kept
cutting and looting
In the morning he felt relieved
They'd cut something off his skull
"We're helping you not exist
Your mother just ate some of your
cerebellum seasoned and nutritious
She's smarter now and more eternal
Her eternity feeds on you"

"I AM YOUR MOTHER LISTEN TO ME IN YOUR MIND
When you were born I sold you to the devil   I feed on you
I raised you for death   I am eternal thanks to you
I took care of you like a little girl   I filled you up
with cuddles and caresses   I made you fragile like glass
so that whenever the time came—And it has!—
you wouldn't fight back
Give in to the pain your companion
for eternity   Since death is eternal
Pain is eternal   You'll hurt forever
And I'll laugh forever"

"I AM YOUR BIG BROTHER" HE SAYS DEEP DOWN
    "I AM ETERNAL
I've fed on you like our mother
We've made blood sausages from your blood
We've eaten your flesh

When you were born you were strong and beautiful and destined
to die   I'll never die   I'm eternal
I'm one of the dark wizards   Our mother
is the greatest witch in the world

Some nights when you're fast asleep
we attack your body and you have no idea
We numb you up and devour
part of your earthly body

You'll wander through death   Your skeleton
will descend to the muddy hell
and choke on the slime"

IN HIS SKULL THE DEAD FATHER'S VOICE THINKING

"Sleep in parks and on sidewalks and paths
I am not dead   The funeral you saw
was an act   I am not buried
They buried a wax doll
Kneel before your executioners   Oh artist
What's a poor artist good for?   For dying
Are you lying in the street?
We threw you far away from us
We loved your big brother
We taught him since he was little
how when and where to be wicked
Wickedness is eternal
We are eternal because we do wicked things
Die far from happiness"

"I AM YOUR SISTER THE WITCH   I AM A WITCH
I am eternal   I know how to do wicked things
Wicked things feed on good things   It's basically helpless"
Hearing his sister the wretched one
foreshadowed a light of goodness:
"Oh sister I've always loved you!
Get the others to forgive me"

The sister answered:
"What can your weak love do for me?
Nothing   I am immortal   I live off your death
I'm not going to ask them to forgive you
since we are wicked to you
Die poor unhappy poor artist
Die and give us eternal life and happiness
All your pain infects us
with great joy
Your pain is our happiness"

LYING ON THE SIDEWALK WATCHING THE STARS

Ragged and starving
An artist
If he could just go back to sleeping on a park bench…
But the kids started throwing rocks at him
He drags himself back toward the park
and finds it empty   Such happiness!
He lies down on a bench   And sleeps

He dreams of paradise   His cousin Lucía
sings with a dreamlike voice   There's a girl
who kisses him and says: "I'm Rafaela   your daughter
I can sing in every language"
She sings in Portuguese and her reddish hair
gets him worked up   She's got black eyes
He feels like he's loved her since the beginning of time

He wakes up crying as it starts to get light

A BUNCH OF KIDS ALL AROUND HIM
They bring him fruit and coffee
One of them has a newspaper
A color photo of him shines on the front page
"Isn't this you sir?" Says a girl
He looks at the photo the bitter smile
Some people relish his exile
He sips the coffee   Nibbles on a mango
"Yeah it's me"
He wishes he could bawl from helplessness
These words he hears deep inside:
"Poor weak artist   Poor poor artist"
We've made millions off this photo
We've sucked the life out of you with this

THE THREAT HAS BEEN CARRIED OUT:

He sleeps out in the open   Sleeps on the street
Night his blanket   Moon his lamp
Stars watch over him
When it gets dark he looks for a place to sleep
Never the same place twice
since neighbors kick him out
Evening search for his bed
A smooth parapet is a luxury   Sweeps the ground
with a torn shirt   His right hand a pillow

Some nights they shoo him away and he goes back
to wandering the darkness like a sleepless comet

"I AM SATAN   YOU ARE MY LEGITIMATE SON
I've given you an easy life comfortable lots of praise
I've let you work with just your fingertips
Celebrated by everyone (even if barely)
Now I surrender you to tragedy and death
Fight back!   Fight back you lazy bum!   Fight back!
Now you're silent   Did you forget the words?
I am Lucifer   formerly the most luminous angel
You are the wretched one   Formerly loved   Formerly spoiled"

"I never knew you existed   As a kid I believed in God   Not in you
Are you really talking to me or have I gone mad?"

"Both   Two undisputed truths"
Silence

"LISTEN TO LEVIÁN THE PAINTER OF ANGELS
You've mocked me so cruelly
Why wretched one   Why?
I curse you too   You'll wander   the face of the earth
The angels will chase after you in my paintings
You will be a spot of sienna
You will be a pebble on the way
My blue angel will watch you with scorn
My violet angel with hate
My purple angel will mock you
No paths when you don't come across them
Scorn   Hate   Mockery for you"

"I AM JESUS THE MAN-GOD
Lying on the sidewalk you're on my back
Wicked one!
Everything you've ever had you stole from me
Lying on the sidewalk you torture me
You rip each mouthful of food from my flesh   It is
unforgivable!   Oh wretched one!
When you die I'll punish your soul
When you die I'll stop suffering a little
Your father Satan will bury you alive
You are the worst man in the universe   That's why
you'll be buried alive all five senses wide awake
I keep suffering on the cross for the people
But one day I'll stop   And you'll
never stop hurting in your grave
You will hurt eternally   Down to your bones"

HE WANDERS IN THE CHAOS OF THE CROWD

Begs for a bite of food   His body hurts
Among the faces he sees someone he knows
The face smiles scornful and mocking
reaches out a hand to offer up the smallest coin
Suddenly he sees the mother dressed up like a queen
buying costly fabrics   The brother at her side
"Mamá!   Mamá!   Hermano!   It's me!"
They don't hear him   Don't see him   Don't respond
They turn the corner and vanish at midday
like an illusion of love

SICK OF CORN HE TAKES SHELTER IN SOME RUINS

It's raining

He looks at his dirty hands in disgust

A poor man hands him clean clothes

"Here your mother sends this for you"

An expensive shirt and linen pants

He bathes without soap against a wall

Almost clean he waits for the wind to dry him off

The man hands him a small copper coin

He struggles to put on the new clothes

The man says to him: "Maybe don't smoke so much hashish"

since it's bad for you "Try to beg with some dignity"

The city dressed in lights waits for him and calls

The nice outfit will be dirty and ragged by morning

DRESSED LIKE THAT NOBODY GIVES HIM
ANY CHANGE

He sees Y at a door to a restaurant
He's surrounded by glowing important women
Y sees him smiles tells him:
My newspaper says you're the best   That makes me happy
You don't know how happy it makes me
Y is a cocky artist nothing special
Surrounded by luxury he's been quick to fame
He comes up to him with a glass of wine   Says:
"You're an artist the best of the best   So drink
I envy you   I'll never make it like you
You were destined to be among the greats   Do you want to
    have dinner with us?
It would be such an honor for us to chat with you
Did you see your front-page photo in my newspaper?
Everyone loves it   Come on   Let's go in"
He lets himself be dragged in by Y   The owner approaches:
"The gentleman can't enter without shoes"

from *The Book of Madness* **(2000)**

DISQUIET IS WHAT MAKES A POET A POET: AN INTERVIEW WITH RAÚL GÓMEZ JATTIN

Víctor Rodríguez Núñez
translated by Katherine M. Hedeen

Months before Raúl Gómez Jattin's death—as Vladimir Marinovich recalls—the residents of Cartagena de Indias would see him "sitting on park benches or lying on the floor of the entrance to the school, dressed in brightly colored shirts and pants, always barefoot." There, day and night, he'd dance, sing, fall in love, hand out nicknames, hurl obscenities, make fun of everyone, "and then he'd get aggressive," grabbing "whatever you were eating, drinking, or smoking."

On the day before he died, Gómez Jattin gave his psychiatrist Adolfo Bermúdez a seahorse, informing him that "they are hermaphrodites." Later, he was taken to jail for a few hours where he picked a fight with some garbage cans and then proceeded to drink all night. At 7:40 the next morning he was hit by a bus. We'll never know if it was suicide, a murder, or an accident. It was May 23, 1997; the poet would have turned 52 a week and a day later; he had been born in the same city on May 31, 1945.

This interview first appeared in a collection of interviews with Latin American poets titled *La poesía sirve para todo*, published in Cuba with Unión Press in 2008.

A few years earlier, this chronicler saw Gómez Jattin behave in the same way on the streets of downtown Medellín, when the editors of the literary magazine *Prometeo* and organizers of the city's International Poetry Festival, with Fernando Rendón at the head, had brought him there to live. Yet, the unnerved (and unnerving) being described above, often the very subject of his own poetry, was not the one I interviewed in a hotel in Antioquia's capital, in the company of Mexican poet José Emilio Pacheco, around 1994. This other man was extremely sweet, gentle, healthy, and, most of all, lucid.

Gómez Jattin spent his childhood in Cereté, a small town in the Colombian Caribbean, the essential space of his poetry. He later studied law at the Universidad Externado de Colombia, in Bogotá, where he became intensely devoted to theater. He then wrote stage adaptations of works by Aristophanes, Swift, Kafka, García Márquez, and Cepeda Samudio. Disillusioned with the experience—for reasons explained later—he returned to the Coast, where he embraced bohemia and poetry.

Gómez Jattin's work shakes the critical scaffolding used to explain his generation and, in general, Colombian poetry from the late twentieth century. It includes: *Poemas* [Poems] (1980); *Tríptico cereteano: Retratos, Amanecer en el valle del Sinú* and *Del amor* [Ceretean Triptych: Portraits, Dawn in the Sinú Valley, and On Love] (1988); *Hijos del tiempo* [Children of Time] (1992);

and *Esplendor de la mariposa* [Butterfly Splendor] (1993). There are three retrospectives of his work: *Antología poética* [Selected Poems] (1991); *Poesía: 1980–1989* [Poetry: 1980–1989] (1995); and *Amanecer en el Valle del Sinú* [Dawn in the Sinú Valley] (2004). This last volume includes the poems he penned in the last moments of his life, titled *El libro de la locura* [The Book of Madness].

As Rafael del Castillo Matamoros points out, Gómez Jattin's poetry returns to "vital instances that had been banned for the sake of […] 'poetic happiness,'" destroying "the limits between poetic and everyday experience," turning to a language that is "casually human: vigorous, naked, precise." Perhaps, ultimately, such poetry implies a "[too] radical attitude," "a critique of existing rhetorical and thematic conventions," "a lucidity that implies getting rid of all the straitjackets for a moment." All these elements are difficult to canonize.

When I interviewed him, Raúl Gómez Jattin had just returned from Havana, where he had been receiving medical attention. As I mentioned above, Pacheco was present during the interview and, at Raúl's and my request, expressed his opinions on several of the issues raised. I have deleted these opinions from the text only to honor the legendary refusal of the notable Mexican poet to be interviewed. I believe that the intervening years have done nothing but add value to the present conversation.

I have for you my good friend
a Sinú River mango heart

Raúl, how did you come to poetry?

I think out of inertia. There was a moment in my life when I was doing university theater—as an actor, playwright, and director, in Bogotá, at the beginning of the '70s—when poetry was a secret vice. I would write for myself and for my closest friends, and then I'd destroy it; those texts were more confessions than ambitions of a serious vocation. Then there was a moment of crisis in Colombian theater; I felt trapped when an extreme politicization invaded the scene. So, I retired to live in a town called Cereté, on the Atlantic Coast, with more than a thousand books of poetry, on my father's small farm.

But I know you've been writing since you were a child...

Not poems; letters, memoirs. My father had always told me that I could be a writer, to take it seriously, but only then did it occur to me to do it for real. I spent eight years reading and rereading poetry from all over the world, everything I had on hand about poetry. The result was that, at the age of thirty-five, I ended up with a group of poems. On one of his visits to the farm, Juan Manuel Ponce, a university friend from Bogotá, read it with surprise and told me it was worth publishing. That was my first book. It had a print run of four hundred copies.

It never got to the bookstores, we just gave it away, but it was well received. It was the first book published by Norma, and it's called *Poemas*.

Publishing a first book at thirty-five is a bit...

Late.

In your vocation as a poet, did anyone object?
Was there something to break with?

Yes. My own ignorance.

Do you feel part of a literary generation?
Do you consider any group of poets as your family?

No, because my contemporaries began to publish ten or twelve years earlier, and they published in the '70s and I began in the '80s. Of course, I feel close to some of them, especially Darío Jaramillo. And I also feel connected to Jaime Jaramillo Escobar, although he belongs to the generation before mine.

For Venezuelan poet Vicente Gerbasi, poetry is something known intuitively, not learned. Do you agree?

Sure. I write blindly. I never try to explain or clarify before I write, only after.

But those eight years you spent on the farm surrounded by books, couldn't they be interpreted as self-study?

Yes, but not for writing. To feed myself spiritually, to know, to have paradigms of poets, not to learn a technique or a way of getting to a poem.

Literary workshops have been in vogue in Latin America since the '60s… Do you believe in the literary workshop?

I have been teaching in them for a few years, but in poetry appreciation workshops. I've never thought that anyone can be taught to write.

Have you done any specific writing exercises?

Yes, I've practiced rhyme. Something very similar to what José Emilio Pacheco mentioned happened to me. I've written lots of sonnets with no intention of getting them published. Before I wrote *Tríptico cereteano*, I spent about six months working with rhyme; just writing, no obligation, knowing that I was doing an exercise. Rhyme appears only occasionally in my poetry, but this practice helped me break free from cheap rhyme and find a rhythm that would help me write. I let go of all that easy crap because rhyme can be vicious.

Jorge Luis Borges declared that rhyme…

Is natural.

> I'm a god in my town and my valley
> It's not because they worship me   But because I do
> Because I bow down before anyone who offers up
> some passion fruits or a smile from their own garden

Edgar Allan Poe maintained that he was able to detail, step by step, how he wrote his poems, and he did so in the case of "The Raven." In other words, he felt capable of being aware of the whole process and even explaining it in a text. Are you?

I'd prefer to talk about how I approach a book of poems, what's going to be a book in the future. I start to write and let the bullshit loose, but I also let go of the light, the fundamental thing, what's going to stay ahead of me. Everything emerges like a kind of matter that's scrambled; it's messy. That's where I choose themes from and then I develop them. Still, there's a part of the process in which verses appear from the world of unconsciousness, from the blank mind. I do nothing premeditated, I write with pure heart, pure feeling, pure inspiration.

But you were just saying that you first visualize the book…

The inner nodule, let's say. Each of the books I've written has a very particular world, a general theme that I develop as I go along. Nothing is premeditated.

Do you rewrite poems after you publish them?

Sure. *Poesía: 1980–1989,* the anthology of my work published by Norma, has corrections, although not very in-depth. For example, I deleted twenty poems from my five books that appear there, and I also made changes to some poems. I do it all the time.

Does a poet need to have discipline, to work systematically?

Naturally. Without discipline, nothing gets done. I don't write every day. The discipline I'm referring to has nothing to do with a temporary, daily routine. It's a discipline of personality, of thinking about poetry, of being permanently committed to the world of poetry, whether through writing or reading or reflection. In my case, and in the experience of many poets, discipline is fundamental, a sine qua non.

In other words, you access chaos through order…

No doubt. It took a lot of hard work and it drove me mad.

Do alcohol and drugs have a positive impact on a poet?

Well, that depends. There was a time when mushrooms opened a window for me. I could see some of my books and I wrote them. The same happened with cannabis. But then they became an obstacle and I stopped.

Now you're in a phase of trying make do without all those kinds of stimulants.

Now I'm working without drugs. I just have a couple of swigs of aguardiente and start writing.

In sober drunkenness...

In the discreet drunkenness of aguardiente.

William Carlos Williams said that poems were mechanical objects made of words to express ideas, feelings.

Mechanical, no. For me poetry is far from being something mechanical. It's something passionate, controversial. There is something in the poem that I struggle with, which I rejoice in, but it's never automatic.

Okay. Let's forget about the words mechanical and automatic. The idea that the poem is a little machine created to express itself, what do you think?

Williams was an American and every American is closely related to the world of machines. Me, not so much.

When you write do you think it's important to set goals, to try to do it like the greats?

I try to write like the best Raúl Gómez Jattin I can be.

Have you ever understood poetry as a kind of refuge, a space where you protect yourself from the world?

As a refuge and also as a watchtower where I send signals from, mostly to poets and those close to poetry. I've given the last twenty-five years of my life to poetry and I have no regrets.

I don't have money or fame, but I have peace of mind; I have managed to live with myself and that seems like a very important achievement.

> Before knocking him down
> Credit the madman
> His clear talent for poetry

According to [Spanish poet] *José María Valverde, poetry has died. What diseases could poetry die from?*

Is José María suggesting that humans have died or that he just feels like he's dead?

The phrase is decontextualized, I'll admit, because Valverde was referring to contemporary Spanish poetry.

Yes, there hasn't been poetry in Spain since [Antonio] Machado.

Charles Baudelaire said that poetry has no other purpose than itself.

I'm not very Baudelairean. I think poetry has an impact ahead of and beyond itself.

Raúl, it's been said that poetry today is less present than in other times. How do you see the situation of poetry in our times?

Well, that depends on where in the world you mean. Film and television, big shows, may have captured the attention of the general public in Western countries, but in Latin America there's a flourishing of reader affection for poets; there's a great capacity for reading. Otherwise, how do you explain the phenomenon we are experiencing, such as these massive festivals in Medellín [referring to the International Poetry Festival in Medellín].

There are people who think that poetry today has less diffusion than in other times, and they blame the breaking down of the border between prose and verse. How do you see the relationship between prose and verse?

Free verse emerged a long time ago and was an early way to get rid of the boundaries between prose and verse. Prose poems are just as valid as poems in verse, whether rhymed, like Borges, or in free verse.

Don't you think that opening up to prose has been harmful to poetry?

No way.

In addition to poetry, you wrote theater for a time…

Yes, but those texts have no importance, I haven't even kept them. They were written for specific stagings; I didn't write them before the staging and then bring them to the stage. They were more like notes about the dramatic movements on stage.

Are there things that cannot be said in verse?

Many, of course. Hence image, music. I mean the universal language of art, which you only see the forms of.

But you haven't had to go beyond poetry, lines on paper.

Since I've been writing poetry, it's enough for me. It's a very large field.

According to [Cuban poet] *Dulce María Loynaz, poetry is a genre of youth, because old people do not procreate. You're leaving youth behind, do you believe that?*

No way. The examples of Borges, of Octavio Paz in our America, show the opposite. Longevity did not prevent them from continuing to produce something new.

As a poet, do you feel committed to something, to someone?

Committed?

Yes.

To writing well.

In Baudelaire, although you don't like him, there's a lot to talk about. He said that the poet loses their strength if they pursue a moral end.

Undoubtedly. I'm never going to try to moralize.

In that sense, are you Baudelairean?

No, I am not Baudelairean. Like I told you, I'm not interested in Baudelaire.

[Cuban poet] *Cintio Vitier has defined the relationship between ideology and literature as an incestuous relationship.*

The word ideology was very fashionable up until a few years ago. I think that ideology is alien to poetic work and the essence of poetry. It is very often present in the same poet, but it is something alien to aesthetics.

> Tonight he'll go to three dangerous ceremonies
> Love between men
> Smoke marijuana
> And write poems

If you had to compile an anthology of contemporary Colombian poetry with not many authors, who would you include?

Ten?

Ten or less.

José Asunción Silva, Porfirio Barba Jacob, Luis Carlos López, Guillermo Valencia...

Valencia? You'd be stoned to death.

I'll take that chance.

Leon de Greiff?

Yes, the Great de Greiff too.

He's not too popular either. I know that young Colombian poets don't like him.

That's their problem. I'd add Álvaro Mutis, Jaramillo Escobar, Giovanni Quessep. The others are my contemporaries, and that is in question.

From el Grupo de Mito, anyone else?

Eduardo Cote Lamus, Jorge Gaitán Durán.

Make sure you haven't left anyone out because later on...

I'll be executed. Aurelio Arturo.

Arturo is the Colombian poet who receives the most attention these days in Colombia. Do you think that attention is really fair?

Aurelio Arturo is a poet who wrote beautiful poems to nature. What I miss in his texts is human conflict, fundamental to the importance of a poet. Of all the Colombian poets I really prefer Mutis.

It seems to me that there is a very marked appreciation of Aurelio Arturo and a very marked devaluation of León de Greiff.

Aurelio Arturo was fortunate enough to write only a few poems, all of very good quality, and León de Greiff hid his good poems in a tidal wave, in those monstrosities as he himself called his books.

The overabundance of León de Greiff...

He's his own worst enemy.

If you had to characterize the current situation of Colombian poetry, what would you say?

I have a very high opinion of it because I'm living it. Yes, I recognize that we are in a good moment.

You were recently in Cuba, for how long?

Five months.

And how did they treat you?

Very well. I was able to recover from a drug problem that was causing me temporary insanity.

Did you have any relationship with [the founder of the psychiatric hospital] *Dr. Bernabé Díaz Ordaz?*

Yes, I had the opportunity to meet him and speak with him, not very long because he is a very busy man who runs such a large and complicated hospital.

So you were there for five months…

In Mazorra [the name used for the hospital].

Do you feel good in this world? Should something change?

That's a very big question, Víctor.

I'll ask again, do you feel good in this world?

Not quite. A poet never feels good. Disquiet is what makes a poet a poet.

Víctor Rodríguez Núñez (b. Havana, 1955) is one of Cuba's most outstanding and celebrated contemporary writers, with over seventy collections of his poetry published throughout the world. He has been the recipient of major awards in the Spanish-speaking region, including, in 2015, the coveted Loewe Prize. His selected poems have been translated into Arabic, Chinese, English, French, German, Hebrew, Italian, Macedonian, Serbian, Swedish, and Vietnamese. In the last decade, his work has developed an enthusiastic readership in the US and the UK, where he has published seven book-length translations. He divides his time between Gambier, Ohio, where he is currently Professor of Spanish at Kenyon College, and Havana, Cuba.

ALMOST OBSCENE: TO RIGHT AND TO WRITE
Translators' Note

Raúl Gómez Jattin (Cartagena, 1945–1997) was one of Colombia's most outstanding writers and the author of seven books of poetry. He remains, arguably, the country's most controversial literary figure and, as such, his work is not easily summarized. He never won any major literary awards, virtually all of his contemporaries continue to shun his work, and critics consider him a total outlier from the national tradition.

*

> I'm about a woman and a man   Broken
> by a tender virility   My soul overpowered
> by a feminality hardened on art

Gómez Jattin wrote in a way no Colombian poet has ever written before, centering on themes that rarely appear in verse from the region: drug use, mental illness, madness, homelessness, unauthorized sexualities, and, for the first time in the Colombian tradition, an openly queer poetic subject. As a queer man of Syrian descent with no formal education in poetry, writing in a way that challenged long-established beliefs about what poetry should be and how poets should act, he was viewed as a threat and his rightful place at the forefront of his country's tradition has long been denied.

I decrypt my hurt with poetry

For Gómez Jattin, poetry is both catharsis and self-destruction: writing becomes an act of existence and resistance against literary and social controls. The themes of his poetry are largely autobiographical: his homosexuality, Middle Eastern heritage, and schizophrenia. These, in turn, contributed to his marginalization both from serious scholarly inquiry as well as from society more generally. He mainly entered the Colombian literary imaginary through an often-sensationalized retelling of his life as an "urban legend" and of the man as a "poète maudit," or, in some circles, the "Caribbean Rimbaud."

*

Dangerous Wretched
Poetry and love did this to me

Born in 1945 and raised in a small town on the Caribbean coast, Gómez Jattin lived, quite literally, on the periphery, far from Bogotá, the country's institutionalized center of cultural production. He spent most of his adult life between psychiatric hospitals, jails, and living as a homeless person. Throughout all of it, he never stopped writing poetry or reciting it on street corners; his instantly famous public readings drew hundreds of listeners. In 1997, he was killed by a bus. It remains unclear if it was an accident, a suicide, or—as the poet's close friends claim—an orchestrated act of social cleansing.

*

I go from hospitals to jails to familiar
  places hostile
like them   Souls with hypodermic faces
and charity beds

Almost Obscene includes work culled from Gómez Jattin's sporadic chapbooks, written from 1980 to 1997, and brought together for the first time in English (or Spanish). We have aimed to provide readers with a representative selection of the poetry. Though the poems we've chosen range widely in content and form, they are united by the uninhibited expression of a marginalized poetic subject and a queerness that not only challenges the heteronormative, but also manifestations of the normative more broadly conceived. There are love poems and philosophical poems, poems with classical references and categorically mad poems, and not one sits neatly at either end of a binary opposition.

*

TO WAKE UP SUDDENLY AT
THE BRINK OF DAWN
sense the devil in the corner of the room

The selection closes with a full translation of his final chapbook, *The Book of Madness*. Published posthumously in 2000, the text documents the poet's final days as he suffered from psychotic episodes and represents one of the rawest, most visceral expressions of severe mental illness to be put into language. The title of this collection, *Almost Obscene*, alludes to what we think is the most appropriate way to define both Gómez Jattin's poetics as well as the precarious position of his speaker: one that unsettles but that cannot simply be written off as "obscene."

*

Poems simple and dreamt-of
grown like grass grows
between the cracks in the pavement

As translators, the great question has been: what to do with the almost obscene? Ironically, the ideas such a description conjures up are far from the reality of these poems. Indeed, much of Gómez Jattin's work is not "indecent" in ways we might expect.

Here, instead of an abundance of avant-garde experimentation or pornographic imagery, there is a sometimes disproportionate amount of overly simplistic sentimentality: commonplace, cliché, greeting-card, ordinary. This questions poetry's limits in a different way: what is in "good taste," what is appropriately poetic. To this degree then, Gómez Jattin's work *is* undeniably obscene. In its earnestness, in its fearlessness, it is just de trop.

*

>I'm not wicked   I just want to make you
>   fall in love with me
>I'm trying to be honest sick as I am

Our translations lean into the overmuch, aiming to privilege volatility instead of stability and to showcase a jaggedness of tone, approach, and mind space, precisely the excessiveness and unpredictability that made Gómez Jattin an uncomfortable presence within conventional Colombian literary circles. In turn, we aspire to challenge narrow US notions of queerness and the imperialist impulse to brand them as a global phenomenon.

*

>these poems of mine I've stolen from death

Bringing Gómez Jattin's work into English has been an urgent task. Everything about this poet and his poetry is underrepresented. Translating him into English is, in part, about what's going on here in the US. It is about representation— widening it, challenging it—especially with regard to conversations around queerness, race, intersectionality, and mental illness, as well as the imperialist view of literature from Colombia. But it is also about what's going on there, in the poet's home country, where Gómez Jattin's work is rarely anthologized, virtually out of print, and rendered a literal footnote in a 600-page history of Colombian poetry. To translate him into English is to continue his fight for recognition, for a place for the perpetually out-of-place. It is to begin to right and write his legacy.

Katherine M. Hedeen
Olivia Lott

Gambier–Mt. Vernon, Ohio
JANUARY 2022

ACKNOWLEDGMENTS

This volume has been compiled from the following titles by Raúl Gómez Jattin:

> *Poemas* [Poems] (1980)
> *Retratos* [Portraits] (1983)
> *Amanecer en el Valle del Sinú*
> [Dawn in the Sinú Valley] (1986)
> *Del amor* [On Love] (1988)
> *Hijos del tiempo* [Children of Time] (1989)
> *Esplendor de la mariposa* [Butterfly Splendor] (1993)
> *El libro de la locura* [The Book of Madness] (2000)

The translators would like to thank the editors of the following journals in which earlier versions of some of these poems first appeared: *Anmly*, *Burning House Press*, *The Kenyon Review*, *Río Grande Review*, and *Words Without Borders*.

Additional thanks to Hilary Plum for her belief in this project and her dedication to it; to the staff at Cleveland State University Poetry Center for supporting our work; to Víctor Rodríguez Núñez for introducing us to Raúl's poetry and for all he has done behind the scenes to make this project a reality; to Ignacio Infante for reading early versions of these translations; to Johannes Göransson for his early championing of this work; and to the community who supports poetry in translation especially Don Mee Choi, Paul Cunningham, Kristin Dykstra, Michelle Gil-Montero, Steve Halle, Joyelle McSweeney, and Jeannine Pitas.

RECENT CLEVELAND STATE UNIVERSITY POETRY CENTER PUBLICATIONS

Edited by Caryl Pagel & Hilary Plum

POETRY

World'd Too Much: The Selected Poetry of Russell Atkins
ed. Kevin Prufer and Robert E. McDonough

Advantages of Being Evergreen by Oliver Baez Bendorf

Dream Boat by Shelley Feller

My Fault by Leora Fridman

Orient by Nicholas Gulig

Twice There Was A Country by Alen Hamza

Age of Glass by Anna Maria Hong

outside voices, please by Valerie Hsiung

In One Form to Find Another by Jane Lewty

50 Water Dreams by Siwar Masannat

Mule: 10th Anniversary Edition by Shane McCrae

daughterrarium by Sheila McMullin

The Bees Make Money in the Lion by Lo Kwa Mei-en

Residuum by Martin Rock

Festival by Broc Rossell

Sun Cycle by Anne Lesley Selcer

Arena by Lauren Shapiro

Bottle the Bottles the Bottles the Bottles by Lee Upton

No Doubt I Will Return A Different Man by Tobias Wray

for a complete list of titles visit csupoetrycenter.com